NULLIFICATION

NULLIFICATION

Reclaiming Consent of the Governed

Clyde N. Wilson

The Wilson Files 2

Produced in the Republic of South Carolina by

SHOTWELL PUBLISHING LLC
Post Office Box 2592
Columbia, So. Carolina 29202

www.ShotwellPublishing.com

Cover: Engraving of "Defence of Fort Moultrie, S.C." by Johannes Adam Simon Oertel, 1858.
Design: Boo Jackson TCB

ISBN-13: 978-0692759769
ISBN- 069275976X

10 9 8 7 6 5 4 3 2 1

PUBLISHER'S NOTE

№ 2 in Shotwell Publishing's series, *The Wilson Files*, collects some of Professor Wilson's writings on State Rights and the timely subject of Nullification, more properly known as State Interposition.   Following the practice of early American discourse, whenever the word "State" appears as a noun referring to one or more of the United States, it herein begins with an upper case "S. Some items have previously appeared in *Chronicles* and on www.lewrockwell.com.

CONTENTS

Jefferson and Nullification 1

Nullification Reconsidered 6

The Real Constitution 9

The 10th Amendment 12

The States Are What We Have 14

The Consent of the Governed Revisited 25

What the Founders Meant 28

What the Founders Didn't Count On 31

The Revolution as Secession 43

Devolution 52

Q & A on Nullification and Interposition 56

About The Author 61

JEFFERSON AND NULLIFICATION

"Resolved, That the several States composing the United States of America, are not united on the principle of unlimited submission to their General Government . . . . and that whensoever the General Government assumes undelegated powers, its acts are unauthoritative, void, and of no force. . . . that the government created by this compact [the Constitution for the United States] was not made the exclusive or final judge of the extent of the powers delegated to itself; since that would have made its discretion, and not the Constitution, the measure of its powers; . . . . that this would be to surrender the form of government we have chosen, and live under one deriving its powers from its own will, and not from our authority; . . . and that the co-States, recurring to their natural right in cases not made federal, will concur in declaring these acts void, and of no force, and will each take measures of its own for providing that neither these acts, nor any others of the General Government not plainly and intentionally authorised by the Constitution, shall be exercised within their respective territories."

SO WROTE THOMAS JEFFERSON, Vice President of the United States, in a document drafted at the request of members of the Kentucky legislature in 1798. Kentucky passed Jefferson's paper and broadcast it to the world as the definitive opinion and stand of the sovereign people of the State. The language drafted by James Madison for similar documents adopted by the Virginia legislature in 1799 and 1800 was similarly unequivocal in its constitutional position and forceful in expression.

The people, acting through their natural polities, the States, had created and given authority to the Constitution of the United States. The Constitution conferred powers on a general government to handle certain specified matters that were common to the "general welfare" of all the States. That government was an agent. It could not be the judge of its own powers. To allow it to be so would mean nothing less than a government of unlimited power, a tyranny. The partners to the Constitution, the sovereign peoples of the States, were the final judges of what they had intended the Constitution to mean. When the general government exceeded its power it was the right and duty of the State to interpose its authority and defend its people from federal acts of tyranny—yes, to render a federal law inoperative in the State's jurisdiction.

1

Clyde N. Wilson

The scholars of the rising leftist Establishment who took over American history writing beginning in the 1930s invented a self-flattering fable to render the Kentucky and Virginia documents themselves null and void. Jefferson and Madison, they said, really did not care about States' rights. They were merely anticipating the great tradition of the American Civil Liberties Union in opposing the Alien and Sedition Acts. Their concern was to defend the freedom of speech of the non-conformist radicals of their time.

This established interpretation is a lie and requires a good deal of ignorance, self-deception, or deliberate falsehood to peddle. It is true that the Virginia and Kentucky acts were not followed up by active resistance to the feds. They did not have to be, because Jefferson and his friends won the following elections, got rid of the bad laws, and compensated those who had been harmed by them. There is evidence that Virginia and North Carolina were quite willing and able to call out the militia if necessary and that grand juries were standing by to indict any offending feds—dealing with them as the Stamp Act agents had been before the War of Independence.

Not interested in State rights? Jefferson reiterated the centrality of State rights to the preservation of liberty and self-government in his inaugural address (and in hundreds of letters for the rest of his life). His party and the succeeding Democratic party proclaimed "The Principles of 1798" repeatedly as their foundational philosophy, right up to the War to Prevent Southern Independence. It could not be clearer: in the American government system State rights and liberty could not be separated. They were the same thing. They had the same defenders and the same enemies. The Sedition Act was not just an invasion of individual rights; it was an illegal invasion of a sphere that the people had left to their States.

Further, the Sedition Act, punishing criticism of federal officials with jail sentences and fines, had been passed in stark defiance of the recently adopted First and Tenth Amendments which absolutely forbade Congress to pass any law abridging the freedom of speech and press and reserved to the States all powers not specifically conferred on the government. How then could Congress pass such a law as the Sedition Act? Because the Federalists, Hamilton and Adams and their supporters, justified their legislation by invoking the Common Law's provisions about the punishment of "sedition." The Common

2

Law existed in each State to the extent that State had found it worthwhile to adopt it, but it had no place in a written document of delegated powers such as the Constitution for the United States. If the feds could ignore specified power limitations by grafting Common Law jurisdiction into the Constitution, then literally everything under the sun could be brought under their power. Not only that, but everything under the sun could be ultimately disposed of by the federal courts, which would become the new sovereign. This had to be stopped.

Interposition by Virginia and Kentucky was intended to halt the Northeastern elite's relentless agenda to become the economic and moral overseers of all Americans through the federal machine. This has always been the engine for the unconstitutional usurpation of federal power—then, since, and now. When State interposition next came into serious play in the United States, the occasion was the tariff laws, by which the Northeastern elite had perverted a constitutional power to raise a revenue into a means of excluding foreign competition and creating a captive market for their profit.

After their service as presidents, Jefferson and Madison lived by their republican ethics—they were private citizens with no special right to interfere in public affairs. But they expressed opinions on issues of the day privately to those who asked and who they trusted. When, less than a generation after the "Principles of 1798" had been proclaimed, the possible nullification of the tariff laws by South Carolina drew attention, Jefferson was gone from the scene. Madison, in contradiction of his own plain language and the circumstances of 1798-1800, claimed that state interposition was not what they had had in mind at that time. Historians who want to trash States' rights and the South Carolina resistance to the tariff during 1828-1833 lean heavily on Madison. Self-evidently, Madison contradicted himself, as he did quite often throughout his career. Unlike Jefferson, he was a superficial and inconsistent thinker who often swung from one side to the other. (That is why his pretentious speculations in *The Federalist,* which, by Madison's own admission, have absolutely no constitutional authority whatsoever, are the favourite text of third string "constitutional lawyers" and would-be "political philosophers.")

We do not have to wonder what Jefferson in his post-presidential years thought about State interposition. It is not in the least a mystery, although it is something of a secret since "scholars" have assiduously avoided exposure of the relevant documents, which are not easy to find. In 1825, the day after his last Christmas in this earthly realm, Jefferson wrote to William Branch Giles, former Senator from Virginia and stalwart Jeffersonian. He shared Giles's concerns about the state of federal affairs. *"I see, as you do, and with the deepest affliction, the rapid strides with which the federal branch of the government is advancing towards the usurpation of all the rights reserved to the States, and the consolidation in itself of all powers, foreign and domestic; and that, too, by constructions which, if legitimate, leave no limits to their powers."*

The minority President John Quincy Adams was pushing a large program of federal expenditures and expanded powers. Adams and his Congressional allies, Jefferson said, for an example, had construed the delegated power to establish post roads into a power to cut down mountains and dig canals. The old, evil program of the Northeastern "monarchists" to enrich themselves off the earnings of the agriculturalists was once again in the saddle. Reason and argument were no good in such a situation. *"You might as well reason and argue with the marble columns"* in the Capitol.

The South might well be forced into a choice between *"the Union with them, or submission to a government without limitation of powers. Between these two evils, when we must make a choice, there can be no hesitation."* However, not yet. *"But in the meanwhile, the States should be watchful to note every material usurpation on their rights; to denounce them as they occur in the most peremptory terms, to protest them as wrongs to which our present submission shall be considered not as acknowledgments . . . ."*

Jefferson mentioned that he had written a letter to Giles on Christmas about important matters, of which Giles "will be free to make use what you please." I have not found this letter, but it probably has something to do with a document Jefferson wrote out on December 24, which he titled "The Solemn Declaration and Protest of the Citizens of Virginia on the Principles of the Constitution of the United States of America and the Violation of Them." It seems to have been intended for the use of Jefferson's neighbours in the grand jury of Albemarle County to begin a program for Virginia once more to interpose, against Congress's usurpation in its "internal improvements" expenditures.

Just three years after Jefferson wrote this, another Vice-President of the United States, at the request of his State, drafted a "South Carolina Exposition," which described the illegality and injustice of the protective tariff and the proper remedy for it: State interposition upon "The Principles of 1798." This "Exposition" was approved and broadcast to the world by the legislature of South Carolina, along with a "Protest." The usual clamour of rent-seekers and petty political operators was raised, claiming, among other things, that Jefferson had not written the Kentucky Resolutions. In 1831 Jefferson's son-in-law produced the draft in the great man's own hand.

There was so much demagoguery broadcast by the opponents of nullification and the shoddy historians who repeat their propaganda, that it is worth saying something about the roles of Jefferson and Calhoun as *drafters* of the Kentucky Resolutions and the South Carolina Exposition. Jefferson, as we have noted, did not publicly acknowledge his authorship. Calhoun's authorship of the Exposition was characterised as an evil, secretive political operation. This propaganda is designed by and for people who can think only in terms of politicians and parties instead of principles and who are ignorant of the ethics of republican virtue that influenced many Americans before Lincoln. Authorship was not acknowledged because it was desired that the statements be understood as the voice of the people of the State, not mischaracterised as merely the position of a national politician.

In a later generation, another minority president seemingly destroyed forever the constitutional role of the States by declaring the open, democratic, deliberative acts of fourteen States to be only "combinations" of criminals who refused to obey him. Lincoln made that stick by a brutal war of conquest that did not "preserve the Union" but changed the Union into a central state with no limits to its power. Those who hope to revive a constitutional role for the States as counters to the present U.S. Empire, must hope to make the States once more into self-conscious, viable polities who have the political will to enact nullification and stand by it.

NULLIFICATION RECONSIDERED

Review: *Nullification: A Constitutional History, 1776--1833*, 3 vols.
by W. Kirk Wood

WITH THE DESTRUCTIVE EVIL of centralised power becoming every day more evident and 10th Amendment resolutions appearing in various State capitals, a look at Professor W. Kirk Wood's magisterial three-volume *Nullification: A Constitutional History, 1776 -1833* is serendipitous.

For the first time in more than a half century and long past due, serious people are beginning to search for ways that the famous "checks and balances" of the American constitutional order might be invoked against a regime which recognizes no limits to its power. Such a search leads naturally to a new look at accepted history and "law." Professor Wood, whose knowledge of the primary documents of early American history is astounding and incomparable, has marshaled overwhelming evidence on the matter.

There is not the least doubt in the mind of any HONEST person who has studied the record, that the preponderance of people who framed and ratified the Constitution intended to form a more perfect Union "for the United States of America," not to establish a United State, a sovereign national power. This understanding was reemphasized in the first Ten Amendments, clearly stipulated restrictions on the powers of the central apparatus. The understanding was sealed in concrete, so people mistakenly believed, when Jefferson and his party took office on "the principles of 1798," the unequivocal declarations by Virginia and Kentucky of their right to block acts of the central government that exceeded its delegated powers.

True, there was an element among the Founders who wanted an unchecked central power. Like every other push for more centralised power since, the primary motive of the Hamiltonians was rent-seeking. But, of course, rent-seekers always portray their agenda as essential for some good purpose—general prosperity, equality, national defense, or some other alleged social good. But so strong was the allegiance to a confederal understanding of the Constitutional regime, that the central power men had to lie about their intentions. In power,

6

Hamilton began to push actions he had argued in the deceitful polemic, *The Federalist*, that the central government would never, ever do.

Professor Wood's evidence is not likely to influence academic historians, political scientists, and law professors. With a few exceptions they are not interested in evidence, only in fashion. False and even childishly superficial arguments about our history and the Constitution flourish today and have long done so. The assertion that Americans' "original intention" was a centralised state has always rested upon coercion, chutzpah, and lies. The most egregious being when Lincoln declared the deliberate, open, democratic, and constitutional acts of secession of the Southern states to be mere "combinations" of criminals too numerous to be arrested by the marshals.

The centralists made a great rhetorical coup when they formed the argument so that their version of the Constitution seems the natural, unquestionable one, and the position of the critics is merely "a compact theory" made up after the fact by bad people for evil purposes. Wood's evidence makes it clear that the opposite was the case. It was the centralists who made up theory *post facto* against established understanding. Their theory was bolstered by semantics and false history. James Madison was not the "Father of the Constitution" but a trimmer who constantly swung from one side to the other and contradicted himself. Which is why he is the hero of every bad historian, "political philosopher," and tyrannical judge in the land. Daniel Webster did NOT win the famous debate with Robert Hayne of South Carolina on State rights. In the Senate and in public opinion Webster was the loser. He became the winner only by subsequent propaganda. South Carolina's bold nullification of the tariff in 1832, against nearly the entire American establishment, is always stated by the historians to be a failure. But it accomplished its purpose—to bring down the rate of taxation.

There is a large American anti-centralist literature, entirely persuasive to anyone who will study it, which of course eliminates most American "scholars." Jefferson, Randolph of Roanoke, Taylor of Caroline, William Rawle, St. George Tucker, John C. Calhoun, Albert T. Bledsoe, Alexander Stephens, and the 20th century work of James J. Kilpatrick, Thomas Woods, William J. Watkins, Brion McClanahan, and Andrew Napolitano, all make an irrefutable case. But never has the evidence been so massively gathered and deployed as in Wood's

7

Nullification: A Constitutional History. He shows an unequaled knowledge of the primary sources and of historians and their errors.

It is good to have this ammunition in our arsenal. An interest in devolution has been modestly flourishing and, it would appear, steadily increasing in recent years. Not only the Tenth Amendment resolutions, but the Free Vermont Republic, the Middlebury Institute, the Abbeville Institute, the Southern National Congress, the Ludwig von Mises Institute, and other groups have achieved what was only a short time ago unthinkable—a serious discussion of checking and even escaping from the jaws of Leviathan by asserting the long dormant power of the people of the States—the multiple sovereigns who created the United States and gave it all the legitimacy that it has. When you speak of secession, devolution, nullification these days you no longer receive derisive hoots but rather looks of serious if puzzled interest.

One of the greatest of American sages and most effective critics of centralised power, John Taylor of Caroline, wrote that States do not have rights. People have rights. States are instruments by which the people may assert their rights against usurpers and oppressors.

Meanwhile, promoters of 10th Amendment resolutions need to understand that the 10th Amendment does not enforce itself. Nor will it ever be recognized by any of the three branches of the central apparatus or existing political parties. It will have to be enforced by the people of the States whose freedom it was intended to protect.

THE REAL CONSTITUTION

THE REAL U.S. CONSTITUTION, which was abandoned long ago, does not permit judges to be its final interpreters. It does not authorise executive orders, coercion of the people of a State by the federal government, delegation of control of the currency to a private banking cartel, the subsidy of private groups and persons, or calling the militia to active service except in case of invasion or rebellion and at the request of the State.

The Constitution's primary function today is to provide lucrative pickings for lawyers and pseudo-respectable cover for power seekers. The central government has no check on its power that is not determined by the politicians in control of its various branches. John Adams's notion that the various branches of the federal machine would check each other is a complete failure. They seldom check each other but frequently check the people and the States. The 14th Amendment, illegitimately promulgated in the wake of Lincoln's revolution, has provided power seekers with everything they need to fulfill their limitless ambitions.

The document that was designed to provide specified operational powers to a federal government is changed into an unappealable instrument of power. There is a great unnoticed peculiarity in the name of this country. Before Lincoln, "United States" was a plural—in all laws, treaties, proclamations, and in the Constitution itself. It was a "Constitution FOR the United States of America." And while Americans sometimes referred to a common identity as a "nation," their common government was usually referred to as the "Union" or the "general government."

We now assume that the Constitution is something to be interpreted by "constitutional lawyers," especially those on the federal bench. "Constitutional lawyers" busy themselves with "emanations" and a "living document," or else they talk about *state decisis* and "original intent." Usually they cite "original intent" from "The Federalist," a series of deceitful essays put forward by the defeated centralist party in the Philadelphia Convention, which was never ratified by any people. The "original intent" of the real Constitution can only be interpreted by the intentions of the people of the States who ratified (gave their consent) and thus made the document valid. Their intentions were made clear by what they said when they ratified and in the clarifying Ten Amendments upon which they insisted. The real Constitution did not belong to lawyers, who obfuscate for a living, but to the people of the States. The proper meaning of the Constitution is not a legal question but a historical one. Citizens do not need lawyers and judges to tell them what THEIR Constitution means. A truly living Constitution would be one in which the people take a continuing and active part in interpretation—as through State Interposition.

Contrary to "democratic capitalists" and other Marxists, economics does not determine history. However, it is regrettably true that money, the love of which is the root of much evil, explains a lot of human motivation. The goal of centralising power in Washington has ALWAYS been part of a wealth distribution agenda. Hamilton and his successors intended to use the government to transfer wealth from the agricultural class to the moneyed class. They even made a plausible defense of this as a patriotic program for national "development."

It was equally true of Lincoln and his Republicans. The PRIMARY accomplishment of his revolution was a permanent national debt and to establish the federal government as the handmaiden of corporations, which has continued to this day. You may deplore or applaud this fact, but it is a fact. It is hardly a secret. Northern leaders at the time said plainly, frequently, and emphatically, that crushing the South was necessary to Northern prosperity. Lincoln's self-contradictory but pretty words about government of the people was window-dressing. Truly, slavery was the most visible issue, though the division over that was not as great as is usually supposed. Plenty of Northerners moved to the South and owned slaves. Without any question Lincoln's goal of forbidding slavery in the territories was not a matter of benevolence toward black people but of keeping the West as the domain of "free white men," i.e., government sponsored capitalists. (The new States created by the Republicans west of the Missouri were not real States but pocket boroughs of the Copper Trust, the Union Pacific Railroad, etc.) The essential cause of the Republicans' war against other Americans was that slave-owning Southerners had too much power and would not get with the self-evidently righteous program of Northern prosperity.

It is the lack of the real Constitution destroyed by Lincoln's violence that today guarantees that the government primarily functions to transfer wealth from the productive classes to the rich and their nonproductive clients. For Lincoln's party the government was a money-making proposition, not a focus of patriotism. That they damaged the real power of the governed was of little concern to the rent-seekers.

Southerners, with their old-fashioned notions of republican virtue and Constitutional limits, were an obstacle to rent-seeking that had to be removed. Karl Marx, many of whose comrades held positions in Lincoln's party and army, completely agreed with Lincoln. The Southerners, who had played a major role in the founding and progress of the United States, were according to Marx an oppressive and aggressive ruling class of "slave drivers" who must be destroyed because they stood in the way of the "labour of the emigrant," i.e., the European national socialist who was to profit from the paradise created by American pioneers. The slave drivers were engaged in a wicked rebellion against the "one great democratic republic whence the first Declaration of the Rights of Man was issued." Lincoln, in the Gettysburg Address, certified and immortalized Marx's version of American history. The meaning of the Constitution had now been re-ordered by ideology and cut off from the people.

Yet the people still have the capacity to exercise power through their indestructible States. State rights is merely an institutional aspect of the primary right of self-government.

THE 10TH AMENDMENT

HEARING SENATOR DOLE babble about the 10th Amendment is a sad reminder—if more evidence were needed—of the terminal ignorance and insincerity of our rulers. But one cannot expect a politician who has been a (very successful) functionary of the imperial state all his life to understand that the delegation of powers by the people has to do with something other than how the (shrinking) pie will be divided up. The 10th Amendment does not have anything to do with who will pay for "motor voter" bills or "free" school lunches or any other of the "benefits" that our rulers provide for the inestimable privilege of serving them. It has to do with a basic function of constitutional government: that is, restraining the abuse of power.

Let us peruse this forgotten relic closely:

The powers not delegated to the United States by the Constitution, nor prohibited by it to the States, are reserved to the States respectively, or to the people.

The amendment is the capstone of those amendments adopted in concluding the process of ratification of the Constitution for the United States. It follows a long list of "shall nots" directed at the federal government and in particular the Congress. More than that, if we are to believe Madison and nearly every other Founder, it provides the fundamental key to construing the Constitution—the Constitution as ratified by the peoples of the States (old and new)—not the opinions of the Philadelphia projectors nor the extra-constitutional musings of "Publius" in *"The Federalist"* so beloved of shallow political philosophers. The Constitution as validated by the consent of the peoples of the States is defined by the 10th Amendment. The federal government, in all its branches, has those powers delegated in the instrument. All other powers are *reserved.*

The great tragedy of American history is that the 10th Amendment is not self-enforcing (else there would have been no need for the previous nine amendments). Various States have and are suing in the federal courts on 10th Amendment grounds against several egregious acts of federal usurpation. This is perhaps to the good as it contributes to educate the public, and a favourable court decision will be helpful. Nonetheless, to ask the federal courts to validate the 10th Amendment is to lose the game before the first whistle. The peoples of the States have not delegated to federal judges the power to decide what their rights are. This is a power they have reserved to themselves.

The 10th Amendment cannot be left up to the federal government for interpretation and enforcement. The essence of Constitutional government is that Power must not be allowed to define its own limits. It must be checked by other Powers. It is up to the States themselves to make the 10th Amendment good, to enforce it by every means at their disposal. The name of this country is, after all, the "United States," a confederation, and not the "American Empire."

THE STATES ARE WHAT WE HAVE

MY SUBJECT IS OUR LOST and stolen heritage of states' rights; my goal is to point out a few home truths that were clear to our Founders and forefathers but that we have lost. Just a few years ago, we had a bicentennial celebration of the Constitution. As far as I am aware, republicanism and federalism, the two most salient features of the Constitution, were never mentioned. Instead, we had a glorification of multiculturalism.

Federalism implies states' rights, and states' rights imply a right of secession. The cause of states' rights is the cause of liberty; they rise or fall together. If we had been able to maintain the real union of sovereign States founded by our forefathers, then there would not be, could not be, the imperial central state that we suffer under today. The loss of states' rights is mirrored by the rise of the American empire, where a vast proportion of the citizens' wealth is engrossed by bureaucracy; where our personal and local affairs are ever more minutely and inflexibly managed by a remote power; where our resources are squandered meddling in the affairs of distant peoples.

That happy old Union was a friendly contract—the States managing their own affairs, joining together in matters of defense, and enjoying free trade among themselves, and indeed, enjoying free trade with the world, because the Constitution, as is sometimes forgotten, required all taxes to be uniform throughout the Union and absolutely forbade taxation of the exports of any State. The federal government was empowered to lay a modest customs duty to raise revenue for its limited tasks, but otherwise had no power to restrict or assist enterprises.

That is what the States United meant to our Founders—happy Union of mutual consent and support. It did not mean a government that dictated the arrangement of every parking lot in every public and private building in every town, and the kind of grass that a citizen must plant around his boat dock. It did not mean the incineration of women and children who might have aroused the ire of a rogue federal police force, unknown to the Constitution and armed as for a foreign enemy. It did not mean that billions would be spent (as in

Kuwait) restoring an oriental despot to his throne. Had George Washington been confronted with these things, he would have reached for his sword.

The founding fathers knew that republican societies were fragile—that they tended to degenerate into empires if extended beyond a small state, though they hoped the federal principle would block this tendency in America. Their definition of self-government was the superiority of the community to its rulers. In a reversal of the age-old pattern of mankind, the rulers (a necessary evil) became delegates of the community temporarily assigned to take care of some part of the public business. In an empire, like the one from which they had seceded, the community existed for the support and gratification of the rulers. A republican America was to be governed in the interest of the communities that made it up; its rulers were "responsible." An empire, to the contrary, was governed by the needs, ideas, interests, even whims, of the rulers. A republic passes over into empire when political activity is no longer directed toward the well-being of the people (mostly by leaving them alone), but becomes a mechanism for managing people for the benefit of their rulers. That is to say, an empire's government reflects management needs, and reflects the desires and will of those who control the machinery rather than the interests and will of those being governed. Who can doubt that we are now an empire? The American people no longer think of the government as theirs, but as a hostile, manipulative, unjust, and unresponsive distant ruler.

A republic goes to war to defend itself and its vital interests, including possibly its honour. Empires go to war because going to war is one of the things irresponsible rulers do. The point of reference for a republic is its own well-being. An empire has no point of reference except expansion of its authority. Its foreign policy will be abstract, and will reflect the vagaries of mind of the rulers, who might, for instance, proclaim that it is their subjects' duty to establish a New World Order, whatever the cost to their own blood and treasure. Who can doubt that the once-proud republican Union of the States is now an empire?

An empire contains not free citizens, but subjects, interchangeable persons having no intrinsic value except as taxpayers and cannon fodder. So, if the governors of an empire should feel that it is easier for them to placate criminals than to punish them, they will turn over the neighbourhoods and schools of their subjects to criminals, and even punish officers of the law for acting too zealously against the criminal class, thus violating the first rule of good government, which is the preservation of order. A people's culture may be changed by imperial edict to reflect a trumped-up multiculturalism (a sure sign of an empire), or their religion persecuted. And, of course, violating one of the essential rules of republicanism, that the laws be equal to all, the imperialists exempt themselves from the commands they lay down for the rest of us. The republican right of self-government and the right of self-determination both necessarily incorporate the right of secession—that a people may withdraw from an imperial power to defend its liberty, property, culture, and faith.

We know the problems. Where should we look for solutions? Changing the personnel of the White House, the Congress, and the Supreme Court has been of little avail. Thomas Jefferson gives us the answer: our most ancient and best tradition, states' rights. In his first inaugural address, Jefferson remarked that in most ways Americans were very happily situated, and then asked:

> What more is necessary to make us a happy and prosperous people? Still one thing more, fellow citizens—a wise and frugal government, which shall restrain men from injuring one another, which shall leave them otherwise free to regulate their own pursuits . . . and shall not take from the mouth of labour the bread that it has earned. This is the sum of good government.[1]

But how to preserve this form of government? What should we do, or not do? Jefferson answered: preserve elections (not the party system), maintain equal justice under the law, rely on the militia, avoid debt, maintain the freedoms of speech, religion, and trial by jury, and avoid entangling alliances. And most important: "the support of the State governments in all their rights, as the most competent administrations for our domestic concerns and the surest bulwarks against anti-republican tendencies."

There is a large sophistical literature which tells us that states' rights was for Jefferson just a temporary expedient for other goals. This is false. For his own generation and several following, it was understood that the state sovereignty of the Kentucky resolutions was Jefferson's primary platform as an American leader. John C. Calhoun, speaking in exactly the same tradition a generation later, said:

The question is in truth between the people and the supreme court. We contend, that the great conservative principle of our system is in the people of the States, as parties to the Constitutional compact, and our opponents that it is in the supreme court. . . . Without a full practical recognition of the rights and sovereignty of the States, our union and liberty must perish. State rights would be found . . . in all cases of difficulty and danger [to be] the only conservative principle in the system, the only one that could interpose an effectual check to the danger.[2]

By conservative principle he means not a political position of right as opposed to left—he means that which conserves and preserves the Constitution as it was intended. Contrast that with our present position. Forrest McDonald, our greatest Constitutional scholar, writes:

Political scientists and historians are in agreement that federalism is the greatest contribution of the Founding Fathers to the science of government. It is also the only feature of the Constitution that has been successfully exported, that can be employed to protect liberty elsewhere in the world. Yet what we invented, and others imitate, no longer exists on its native shores.[3]

Why are states' rights the last best bulwark of our liberties? It is a question of the sovereignty of the people—in which we all profess to believe. Every political community has a sovereign, an ultimate authority. The sovereign may delegate functions (as the States did to the federal government) though it may not alienate authority. It may not always rule from day to day, but it is that place in the society that has the last word when all else is said and done.

All agree that in America the people are sovereign—we are republicans, not monarchists or aristocrats. But what people? The term is not self-defining, any more than is the term liberty. What do we mean by the people? How do we know when the people have spoken? A simple electoral majority, which can shift the next day, is insufficient in bottom-line questions of sovereignty. By people, do we mean that if a million Chinese wade ashore in California and out vote everybody else, then they are sovereign? I think not.

In American terms, the government of the people can only mean the people of the States as living, historical, corporate, indestructible, political communities. The whole of the Constitution rests upon its acceptance by the people acting through their States. The whole of the government reflects this by the representation of the States in every legitimate proceeding. There is no place in the Constitution as originally understood where a mere numerical majority in some branch of the federal government can do as it pleases. The sovereign power resides, ultimately, in the people of the States. Even today, three-fourths of the States can amend the Constitution—that is, they can abolish the Supreme Court or the income tax, or even dissolve the Union. In no other way can we say the sovereign people have spoken their final word. States' rights is the American government, however much in abeyance its practice may have become.

The alternative to State sovereignty, as Calhoun pointed out, is to give the final say-so to the black-robed deities of the Court, who go into their closets, commune with the gods, and tell us what *our* Constitution means and what orders we must obey, no matter how absurd their interpretation may be. But this is to abandon the sovereignty of the people, that is, to abandon democracy or republicanism and to abandon constitutional government for oligarchy—and for an oligarchy based upon mystification rather than reason. James Madison, thought to be the Constitution's father, tells us that the meaning of the Constitution is to be sought "not in the opinions or intentions of the body which planned and proposed it. but in those of the State conventions where it received all the authority which it possesses."[4] *All the authority which it possesses!*

The sovereignty of the people, in which we all claim to believe, can mean nothing except, purely and simply, the people of each State acting in their sovereign constitution-making capacity—as they did in the American Revolution when they threw off their king and assumed their own sovereignty, making their own constitutions. This was a revolution in the sense of a transfer of the locus of sovereignty, not in the sense of social upheaval. The people of each State ratified the Constitution as freely consenting sovereigns, agreeing to make an instrument, limited and precise, for some of their common business.

The case of South Carolina is illustrative but not unusual. The people of South Carolina were sovereign and independent before the Declaration of

Independence. Through their own governor, legislature, courts, and armed forces they were exercising every sovereign power—taxation, war, treaty-making, and the execution of felons. The week before the Declaration of Independence, Colonel Moultrie and the South Carolina forces, from their palmetto log fort on Sullivan's Island, repulsed and defeated a British fleet that threatened to suppress their sovereign self-government.

The question is not altered by the fact that the Union has been expanded to fifty states. The Founding Fathers wisely made the Union expansible. The Congress may *admit* new states (or not), but the federal government does not *create* new States. States create themselves. The federal government may administer the territory, the land, before statehood, but only the sovereign people can adopt a constitution and incorporate themselves into a political society. Only by a sovereign act of free consent can a State ratify the U.S. Constitution—if we believe in government of the people. This is as true of the new States as the old, of Montana as of South Carolina—if we believe the people are sovereign.

Americans are natural republicans, not monarchists or aristocrats. That is, we believe government rests upon consent of the governed—this is the key phrase of the Declaration of Independence. Government is legitimate in just so far as it rests upon consent, that is, the people accede to the government. The opposite of accede is secede—the withdrawal of consent. The right to self-government rests on the right to withdraw consent from an oppressive government. That is the only really effective restriction on power, in the final analysis.

The American Revolution was not seen by our Fathers as a one-time event after which we were bound forever by the government. Of course, they did not wish to encourage so decisive a proceeding as secession for "light and transient causes," but it remained, in the final analysis, an option. Jefferson referred specifically to the "secession" of the colonies from Britain, and he was willing to entertain the idea that in the future there might be two or more confederacies among the Americans (just as there had been many states and confederacies among the freedom-loving Greeks). The point was to preserve the right of self-government. What was sacred was not the Union but the consent of the governed, to which the Union might or might not be of assistance. Jefferson and the other Founders were patriots, not nationalists.

Anyone who has studied, with any degree of depth and honesty, the founding years and the period which followed understands that the idea of states' rights was considered obvious by our forefathers, however wildly irrelevant it may seem today. Centralisers were always on the defensive, and always compelled to conceal their intent. The United States were universally spoken of in the plural. It was clearly understood that the Bill of Rights meant the States binding the federal government to stay out of certain areas. ("Congress shall make no law. . . .") To most people at the time, and for several generations thereafter, the electoral victory of Jefferson and his friends in 1800 meant primarily the putting to rest of a too-assertive idea of national power. General Hamilton was sent home and his schemes of centralisation were put to rest, and so it remained until the War Between the States. But even that, though it fatally compromised the idea of states' rights, did not destroy it.

The states' rights interpretation of the Constitution was not, as its enemies have alleged, a mere theoretical rationalisation made up for the defense of slavery. It is, rather, a living heritage of great power, absolutely central to the understanding of the American liberty. It was the fundamental issue of the most bloody war in which Americans have been involved. Lost and stolen as the idea may be, American history cannot be understood without it. Alexis de Tocqueville, the French historian thought by many to be the most profound foreign observer of America, wrote this in the 1830s:

> The Union was formed by the voluntary agreement of the States; and these, in uniting together, have not forfeited their nationality, nor have they been reduced to the condition of one and the same people. If one of the States chose to withdraw its name from the contract, it would be difficult to disprove its right to do so.[5]

Tocqueville was merely expressing what everyone already knew.

Lord Acton, the great British historian who devoted his life to the study of liberty and to what was conducive to and inimical to the establishment and preservation of liberty, wrote shortly after the war that the defeat at Appomattox was a greater setback for genuine liberty than Waterloo had been a victory. Waterloo ended an empire; Appomattox established one. Acton wrote also:

> The theory which gave to the people of the States the same right of last resort against Washington as against Great Britain possessed an independent force of its own, northern statesmen of great authority maintained it, its treatment by Calhoun and Stephens forms as essential a constituent in the progress of democratic thinking as Rousseau or Jefferson.[6]

Here is a very simple proposition that our forefathers understood—that indeed governed everything they did. The only way to preserve civil liberty is to check government power. The only way to check power is to disperse and divide it. Some of the Founders hoped that a federal system would allow growth without centralisation (or "consolidation" as they called it). This, the main check, has failed. It was also hoped that the division of legislative. executive, and judicial power in the general government would help. Let us be clear—these checks and balances do not work. They ceased to work a long time ago. The Supreme Court does not check the Congress, or the President—it checks us. There is no serious conflict of power among the federal branches. The acts of all of them are directed toward checking the people of the States.

The federal government will never check itself—that is the *raison d'etre* of federalism. It must be checked by the States. And this ultimately is of no avail unless it is backed by the right of secession. Curiously, recognition of the right of secession often obviates its use, because where it is a real possibility, power is motivated, has incentive, to check itself and be responsible.

Federalism is one of the least understood, both theoretically and practically, of all political forms. The habit of not even thinking about it, as in the Constitution bicentennial, provides a great obstacle, which there are signs today of a tendency to overcome. We must beware of phony forms of top-down federalism that will be invented by cornered politicians. Federalism is not when the central government graciously allows the States to do this or that; that is just another form of administration. True federalism is when the people of the States set limits to the central government.

States' rights has fallen into disuse not because it is unsound in history, in constitutional law, or in democratic theory. It remains highly persuasive on all these grounds to any honest mind. It has fallen into disuse because it presented the most powerful obstacle to the consolidation of irresponsible power—that consolidation which our forefathers decried as the greatest single threat to liberty. For that reason, states' rights had to be covered under a blanket of lies and usurpations by those who thought they could rule us better than we can rule ourselves. At the most critical time, the War Between the States, states' rights was suppressed by force, and the American idea of consent of the governed was replaced by the European idea of obedience. But force can only settle questions of power, not of right.

States' rights are historically sound, constitutionally sound, ethically sound, and sound from the point of view of democracy. Where they fall short is simply in the realm of political will and agenda—the practical effort to implement them. That can change.

The people of the States have a *right* to protect themselves against an out-of-bounds federal government, and to determine when the proper bounds have been passed and to interpose their sovereignty, as Jefferson said, as Madison said, as Calhoun said. Proclaiming a right, of course, does not make it prevail. For a long time now, more than a century, the course of history has been moving in the direction of consolidation, the gathering of concentrated power in one central, irresponsible, imperial government. But there is hope. We now see, all over the Western world, a ferment of people against consolidation, in favour of regionalism, devolution, secession, breakup of unnatural states, and the return to historic identities in preference to universal bureaucracies. You know the signs in the break-up of the Soviet Union and Czechoslovakia, and you can see the signs in the secessionist movements in Britain. Italy, Canada, and many other countries.

There is reason to believe that the consolidation phase of history may be coming to an end. We may be ready for a new flowering of freedom for families and communities. We know that the great periods of Western history have been not those of powerful states but of multiple and dispersed sovereignty—flourishing liberty for small communities. We know that such freedom equals creativity in wealth, art, intellect, and every other good thing. All over the

Western world once again people are thinking of liberty—the most characteristic and unique of Western values—and are doubting the central state that has been worshipped since the French Revolution.

I know there are many moral and social problems that are not solved by political arrangements, and that the level of statesmanship in the States is not much higher, if at all, than in the federal government. But if we are to speak of curbing the central power, the States are what we have got. They exist. They are historical, political, cultural realities—the indestructible bottom line of the American system.

It would be a shame if, in this world-historical time of devolution, Americans did not look back to an ancient and honourable tradition that lies readily at hand. To check power, to return the American empire to republicanism, we do not need to resort to the drastic right of revolution nor to the destructive goal of anarchic individualism. We have in the States ready-made instruments. All that is lacking is the will. Our goal should be the restoration of the real American Union of sovereign States in place of the upstart empire under which we live.

---

[1] *The Life and Selected Writings of Thomas Jefferson,* Adrienne Koch and William Peden, eds. (New York: Modern Library, 1944), pp. 323-324

[2] *The Essential Calhoun,* Clyde N. Wilson, ed. (New Brunswick, NJ: Transaction, 1992), pp. 299-302

[3] Forrest McDonald, *Requiem: Variations on Eighteenth Century Themes* (Lawrence: University Press of Kansas, 1989)

[4] *Writings of James Madison,* Gaillard Hunt, ed. (New York: Putnam, 1900 -1910), vol. 9, p. 372

Clyde N. Wilson

[5] Alexis de Tocqueville, *Democracy in America* (New York: Vantage, 1990), vol. 1, pp. 387-388

[6] *Selected Writings of Lord Acton* (Indianapolis: Liberty Press), pp. 170-171, 363

THE CONSENT OF THE GOVERNED REVISITED

Review: *A Constitutional History of Secession*
by John Remington Graham

AMERICANS HAVE LOST the habit of constitutional government. Judges hand down commands derived from their own personal revelation, in the teeth of law and majority rule, and are tamely obeyed by millions. A President sworn to uphold the Constitution of the United States commits the blood and treasure of the citizens in war against a distant state that has provoked his personal ire or the dislike of his unelected entourage. Another President proceeds in his goal "to remake America," something that is nowhere listed in his constitutional powers.

To have lost constitutional government is to have lost self-government, Self-government has apparently come to mean no more than counting up punch-card holes to determine which of two interchangeable celebrities will preside over the immense, unreachable, and unlimited machinery on the Potomac that can take our property and even our lives in a fit of pique or even of absent-mindedness. But note: The Founding Fathers in the Declaration of Independence spoke not of throwing the rascals out to make way for another bunch of rascals; they spoke of resisting a government that had forfeited the consent of the people.

Much of the problem results from the inclination of too many Americans to conflate the state apparatus and the people, to fail to distinguish government from society. Thus, people say "New York City is broke," though the statement does not apply to the place and the people, in all their multifarious life, but only to the passel of politicians who locally monopolize the powers of taxation and legal deadly force. Thus, many Americans seem to regard the President—any president—as a benevolent uncle (the way many Russians viewed Uncle Joe), as a fountain of good will and competence who can do no real wrong and make no serious mistake. After all, we are one big. happy family that plays together.

For the Founding Fathers—or, at least, for the better part of them—the entire point of constitutional government was to provide means for the people to restrain the office-holders. These office-holders were not coterminous with the existing human society but delegates who needed to be kept from overreaching the authority the people had given them. Politicians were, unfortunately, a necessary evil. Like all the rest of us sons and daughters of Adam, they were vessels of vanity, greed, and lust with a perpetual temptation to take advantage of their position. A constitution set limits to help ensure that rulers protected society rather than preyed on it.

John Remington Graham has gone back to the origins of our self-government and has found them in the same place the American statesman of independence found them—in England's Glorious Revolution of 1688-1689, with a nod further back to Magna Carta. The society of England changed the form of its government by casting off the legitimate Stuart monarch and establishing a new royal house with the consent, and on the terms, of the society. In Graham's words, "the occasion was revolutionary, and it was also lawful, peaceable, bloodless, orderly, necessary, beneficial, and glorious." On the same principle the 13 North American colonies changed their form of government by an act of constitution-making by the sovereign people: dissolving their allegiance to the British Crown, creating 13 constitutional republics, and later giving their consent to a mutual agreement in the Constitution for the United States. Another name for this is *secession:* the withdrawal of consent from the existing form of government. As Graham puts it:

> The right is universal, rooted in natural law and legal tradition—a right of peaceable and lawful revolution . . . . It is a right necessary in extraordinary circumstances for every free and civilized people, whatever their race or culture, wherever their location in the world, whenever they have entered into federal relations with neighbouring peoples for mutual advantage. Without it, federal relations are too dangerous to consider. With this right, federal relations can be a great blessing to mankind, and can assure peace and friendship among nations.

Graham brings to the question his considerable knowledge of law and history, a great power of synthesis, and—perhaps most importantly—the experience of his participation in the *amicus curiae* brief for the judicial proceedings in the Canadian high court on the rights of Quebec. The case of Quebec serves as a model of a society claiming and receiving the right to protect its own peculiar qualities from a central power in control of a potentially hostile majority. Would that Americans had as much allegiance to their own Constitution and tradition. Unfortunately, we seem more intent on constructing a police state manned by bully-boy *federales* who regard criticism of "our President" as treason and who are far more adept at murdering dissident citizens than at protecting us from foreign enemies. Nevertheless, there are signs, as in Graham's work, that some of us are beginning to emulate the Founding Fathers and to think about the legitimacy of forms of government.

WHAT THE FOUNDERS MEANT

Review: *The Founding Fathers' Guide to the Constitution*
by Brion McClanahan

THE FEDERAL CONSTITUTION ratified by the people of the States provided for a limited government to handle specified joint affairs of the States. The document describes itself not as "the U.S. Constitution" or the "Constitution of the United States," but as a "Constitution FOR the United States of America." With this in mind, read what follows in the preamble as the purposes of this instrument: "forming a more perfect Union," "common defense," and "general welfare." Throughout the document "United States" is a plural (the States United) and treason against the United States consists of levying war against THEM.

As clear and simple as these facts are and have always been, grasping them seems to be beyond the abilities of presidents, congresspersons, supreme court justices, and professors of "Constitutional Law" at the most prestigious institutions.

In recent times the abuses of these people (what the Founders would have described as "usurpations" justifying rebellion) have run amuck, distorting an already wounded Constitution beyond recognition. Ambition, rent-seeking, willful historical ignorance, deceit, ideology, and the lust for power (which the Founders hoped to guard against) have rendered the real Constitution of our forefathers virtually null and void.

A recent contribution (among a number) to the enterprise of recovery of the authentic Constitution is *The Founding Fathers' Guide to the Constitution* by Professor Brion McClanahan. McClanahan's treatment of the subject makes for a concise, hard-hitting constitutional handbook that goes right to the true source of understanding without being diverted by later commentaries and judicial opinions. What the drafters of the Constitution meant is revealed by their discussions and votes, including the ideas that were voted down. (Many of those reappeared later touted as legitimate federal powers.)

James Madison is reputed by those who don't know any better to be the "Father of the Constitution." In fact, Madison lost more votes than he won at Philadelphia, although he did more maneuvering and scribbling than any other delegate. In his almost half-century of post-ratification life Madison was all over the place, contradicting himself numerous times on constitutional interpretation. But Madison himself in one of his more lucid moments tells us where we should look for the meaning of the Constitution. The meaning of the Constitution, he avowed, is to be found in the understanding of those who ratified it, who alone gave what was merely a proposal all the authority it possesses.

So we must look for understanding at the discussions that preceded the ratification conventions and at the conventions themselves. McClanahan knows this ground thoroughly and tells us in convincing chapter and verse on each Article what those who ratified the Constitution intended and, perhaps more importantly, what they did not intend.

The opponents of the Constitution feared that the document would prove an instrument for the incremental establishment of a centralised dictatorship over the people. They were right. But, as McClanahan makes clear, the proponents of the Constitution swore point by point that the powers granted were limited and no cause for alarm. (We must conclude that either they were mistaken or were acting in bad faith.) These assurances persuaded some of the doubtful. Ratification would never have passed otherwise, and, as it was, it only passed with assurances that amendments would be swiftly adopted and with several States making it clear that their ratification was revocable.

So in interpretation we ought to be guided by what the proponents of the Constitution plainly said it intended. This is what McClanahan elucidates point by point. If we accept what its proponents said, then those who ratified it believed that it established a limited federal power. Third-string "political philosophers" and "Constitutional scholars," and even learned jurists, have made an icon out of *The Federalist,* but it is only one of many discussions of the Constitution. It was a partisan document designed to overcome the objections of New York, and was not very convincing to its audience since ratification passed in New York by the narrowest possible margin. Furthermore, it discusses the Constitution as it was merely a proposal under consideration and not the

Constitution as ratified by the people of the States, who made their intentions clear in the undisputable language of the 10th Amendment. The authors— Madison, Hamilton, and Jay—were all disappointed that the Constitution did not centralise power as much as they would have liked, yet realized what they had to say to win over the majority. On the part of Alexander Hamilton, contributions to *The Federalist* were outright dishonest, because once he got into power he worked to do all sorts of things that he claimed the Constitution did not authorise.

The Federalist, which we see cited all the time as the key to the Constitution, is speculation and was never ratified by anybody. But handicapped thinkers read Madison's philosophical ruminations, nearly all of which have been proved superficial and wrong, and imagine themselves participating in deep thoughts about government and learning about the true Constitution. This is part of the long-established practice of treating the Constitution as something sacred handed down by divine wisdom rather than understanding it by its real history.

The Constitution is there. It can still be known and understood by honest citizens, albeit with many obstacles to be overcome. As McClanahan writes, the real Constitution is a "limiting document," not a grant of limitless power. Whether that Constitution can ever be established again is a question of political will and whatever is left in the American people of a capacity for self-government.

WHAT THE FOUNDERS DIDN'T COUNT ON

EVEN IF WE DO NOT subscribe to an "evolutionary" rendering of the Constitution (as opposed to "original intent"), we are forced to recognize that the Constitution has a history. Besides many lesser scars, it carries on its face the great and bloody gash of Civil War and Reconstruction, an unparalleled social upheaval which was in its essence a question of constitutional interpretation. Even if, carried away by the warm glow of patriotism, we can put aside the complications of history, still, we are confronted with a Constitution that means different things to different people—things that are sometimes mutually exclusive.

The Framers and several subsequent generations of Americans were fond of days of public prayer and thanksgiving. (Even that majority who, contrary to what some would tell you, were not Puritans.) Such would provide a proper way to celebrate the Constitution. We could reflect on our legacy, and rather than wallow in self-congratulation, could perhaps consider how we could better be worthy of it. But alas, our brilliant legal minds have recently discovered that the Constitution has "evolved" so as now to prohibit public religious observances.

It is curious that the more our rabid secularists exclude genuine religion from public life, the more permeated with pseudo-religious emotion public life becomes. The people who exclude prayer from public schools are the very same people who whip up and profit from a misplaced religious emotion for the late Kennedy brothers and the late Dr. King. This is to turn the Founding Fathers on their heads, for they would neither have excluded religion from public life nor deified common human beings. And would have considered either tendency dangerously anti-republican.

Opposing the Bork nomination to the Supreme Court in 1987, someone wrote to the "Letters" column of *Time:* "His reliance on original intent precludes the notion that the Founding Fathers originally intended us to evolve as a people into something better than we were. The nation, and indeed the

31

President's legacy, would be better served by a Justice who views the Constitution as a living part of the present rather than a relic from the past."

This passage encapsulates a vast region of mischief and misunderstanding. A few obviously political points can be made: Would we be a better people by having more abortions? by executing fewer murderers? by having fewer prayers in fewer places? by oppressing more people with reverse discrimination? But it is more interesting that the letter-writer does not reject "original intent." Indeed, logically, no one can. Rather he has supplanted the "original intent" of the written Constitution with an imagined "original intent" of the Founding Fathers for us to "evolve as a people into something better than we were." Those realistic republicans, the Framers, skeptical of human nature and anxious to construct a power that was both effective and limited, content with compromise, have been converted into a priestly caste who bequeathed to us a secret mission of evolving into better beings.

This appeal to the higher law is legally, logically, and historically an absurdity. It traces back not to the Founding but to transcendentalism, which was a 19th century vulgarization, by a small but influential group of Americans, of German philosophy. Thomas Carlyle took Ralph Waldo Emerson around the London slums again and again, but he could never make him believe in the reality of the Devil. This letter-writer could be taken around history again and again but could never be convinced that the Framers did not share his aspirations. They were sensibly hopeful men and principled republicans, which is not the same as devotees of national "evolution."

This confusion of the Constitution with some sort of subjective higher law, one way or another, is nearly pervasive among both the "liberals" and the "conservatives," though it takes different forms at different times. Though a good deal more clever and circumstantial about it, the faculty of the Harvard Law School (and thus the Supreme Court for the last 50 years or more) present essentially the same view of the Constitution. They have read into it an intent, or at least a natural tendency, to evolve into meanings that establish their preferences for social change. The Constitution evolves, but only in the direction *they* say. Although evolution is presumably by definition open-ended, it cannot evolve in directions they do not approve of, even if such an evolution is compatible with its letter and history. The Supreme Court is supposed to read

32

the election returns, but only if the returns turn out their way. Once the Court has discovered something in the Constitution, no one else is allowed to discover something that contradicts it—a curiously limited and controlled form of evolution. Thus there is a federal right to prevent the States from *prohibiting* abortions, but there can be no federal right to prevent the States from allowing them. In fact, both propositions are nonsense because in the real "original intent" of the Constitution (even with the 14th Amendment added) abortion is not a matter in which there is any federal power, nor any judicial power except in the most limited sense.

Anyone who has honestly and closely studied the Founding years and the period that followed knows how large state rights loomed in the understanding of the Constitution in those days. Although there was some disagreement, some ambivalence, and even a few cases of disingenuousness among the Founders about the locus of sovereignty, there can be no doubt that most of the Founders and the subsequent two or three generations of statesmen accepted as natural and right the broadest possible idea of State rights. To most of the Founding generation, the Bill of Rights meant primarily a binding of the federal government by the States. To most people of the time, the victory of Jefferson and his friends in 1800 signified primarily the defeat of a too assertive federal power. Throughout the first half of the 19th century, the absolute central principle of the Jeffersonian Party and of the Democratic Party which came along later was state rights—the principle that the States were the truest representatives of the people's will and the best guardians of the people's liberty. And this belief was matched by democratic sentiment—the more faith one had in the people the more allegiance one gave to state rights. As recently as 1932 the Democratic Party went on record against the dangers of an overextended federal government.

What would the Founders, or indeed anyone before 1932, have made of a situation in which the States have all but disappeared except as administrative units and electoral counters of the federal machinery? And all in the name of freedom and the rights of the individual? Today the federal government, and usually the unelected parts of it, determines the qualifications of the voters and the apportionment of the legislatures of the States. It determines the curriculum and student assignments of their public schools, the rules of proceedings in their criminal courts, the speed limits on their highways, and the arrangement of parking spaces at their public and private buildings. We observe the strange spectacle of legislatures *required* to pass laws according to specifications drawn up by federal judges and federal bureaucrats, which, of course, is not lawmaking at all. The States may have larger budgets and do more things than ever before, but their constitutional authority has never been lower. In the perspective of American history or of the Founders, this is an absolutely amazing development which has hardly been noticed.

The appeal to federally guaranteed individual rights as the chief (evolutionary) feature of the Constitution is essentially antidemocratic. It takes the Constitution away from the people, whose Constitution it is, and gives it into the keeping of an elite class that considers itself the master of mysteries that no majority, either state or federal, can tamper with. It is not the dead hand of the past ("a relic from the past") that the advocates of an evolutionary Constitution fear. What they fear is the restraining hand of the people's will.

An evolutionary Constitution implies a path of evolution, either inevitable or actively pursued. But who is to discern the path? We have a guardian class of savants privileged to lead the way. The status of such tyrants rests not on talents or public services but on claims to special revelation. In other words, they are not republican delegates of the people but priestly oracles—what the Founders would have immediately seen to be clever usurpers and to us hardly distinguishable from the vanguard of the proletariat.

It is true that majorities can be wrong and that minorities have indefeasible rights enshrined within the spirit of the Constitution. But make no mistake, our elitist interpreters and molders of the Constitution are not talking about the rights of minorities to be defended and to defend themselves. They are talking about the rights of a minority, themselves, to rule, to be the sovereign, the ultimate authority. And this theory has become a fact.

It is a curious truth that those who claim rationality, the liberals, with their permanent revolution and reliance on the supposedly objective spirit and findings of social science, always resort to the most irrational view of the Constitution—on the one hand to a mystical and disembodied appeal beyond the letter, and on the other to the most petty and deceitful manipulations of the plain sense. The obvious result is to remove the Constitution from the people and have it perform as a cover for elitism.

But in fact, the Constitution, properly considered, does not give any rights at all. An essential characteristic of a written constitution is that it embodies limitations on government. The people establish institutions and give up to them certain powers, and no more. The government is not presumed to give the people their rights; and indeed the Bill of Rights is cast in a negative form: "The Congress shall make no law . . ." That is, our rights are not a grant from the federal government, and the chief duty of the federal government is to refrain from interfering with them and leave to our real communities their day-to-day definition and application. By this analysis, all that the 14th Amendment "intended" was to make the freed men citizens.

There is a certain liberal spirit, genuinely American and legitimately derived from Jefferson, which says that the earth belongs to the living generation, which must be free to make its own arrangements. But our constitutional evolutionists represent the exact opposite of this spirit—they represent not a forthright amendment by popular consent (which can be completely compatible with the spirit of traditions and institutions) but an essentially rigid and disguised manipulation of the existing Constitution.

I have said that the appeal over the Constitution to the higher law is pervasive. For example, I have before me a *Reader's Digest* (Sept. 1987) containing the reflections of the former Chief Justice Burger on how our Constitution should be viewed and celebrated in its bicentennial. It is impossible to imagine anything more "mainstream." I set aside the silliness of the title, "The Birth of a True Nation." Was the United States an "untrue" nation before the Constitution? I quote the blurb, which is not the language of Burger but is a not-unfair representation of his sentiments expressed on this and other occasions: "Two centuries ago in Philadelphia, one of the most extraordinary events in all human history occurred, and America and the world were thereby transformed." This from one whose duty is presumably a sober application of the law.

The framing of the Constitution was a remarkable event, but I will have to reflect a little on the invention of the wheel and the appearance of Jesus before conceding "one of the most extraordinary events in all human history." Further, the Constitution was not a unique event but a part of a series of events which ought to be understood not as "a Miracle at Philadelphia," to quote the title of a popular work. The Constitution becomes a mysterious act rather than a realistic human achievement. Every clause of the *Digest's* statement is, in fact, a falsehood. One does not know whether the pseudo-religion or the pseudo-history is more odious.

America was not transformed *by* the Constitution, except in a limited sense that a new governmental machinery was launched for the Union of the States. It remained the same society, essentially, as it had the year before. The Constitution did not create republicanism, which had already been created by the people of the States as the first step in the Revolution. It did not create the idea of the written constitution, which also had already been done by the States, which is why John Adams wrote his *A Defence of the Constitutions of the United States.*

But we have here not only America transformed but also the *world!* Now it is true that the Founders sometimes appealed to Mankind. However, they did not deal in emotions, ideologies, and fantasies, but principles. They had a modest hope that by the successful operation of republican principles they might provide an example and inspiration for other peoples. Nothing could have been further from them than the spirit of making the world "safe for democracy." If someone had blathered "global democracy," the official rhetoric of the chosen intellectuals of recent Presidents, to General Washington, he would have reached for his sword. "Global democracy," in specific historical terms, goes back to the 1930s, when it was created as a mélange of Wilsonism and Soviet popular front propaganda. Given the propensity of American governments for dropping high explosives on the "enemies of democracy," such propaganda can do nothing today but make every intelligent foreigner feel uneasy and render prudent discussion of the national interest nearly impossible. In the past 40 years, a great achievement in the founding of government for Americans becomes a cover for the fantastic delusions of "conservative" politicians and intellectuals for world transformation.

I am less offended by the factual license of the ex-Chief Justice's blurb than I am by its spirit. The *tone* is all wrong. It smacks of a spoiled child congratulating himself on Daddy's riches. The Framers, I believe, would not want to be worshiped as workers of a miracle. What they would want is the "decent respect" of sensible men for the hard-won achievements of their fathers.

To treat the accomplishment of the Philadelphia Convention as though it were a manifestation of divine intervention in history is to avoid understanding to what degree it was an accomplishment of the American people and the American leadership class as they then existed in the historical opportunity that they were given. The Framers were giants because they were wise and responsible representatives of the American political fabric of the time. The Constitution was not a miracle or even a piece of good luck. It was an achievement that grew out of the experiences and virtues of Americans of that day.

After all, some of the best men were not even in Philadelphia. There were leaders in the ratification conventions on both sides equal in abilities to the Framers, and most States could have fielded several delegations of equal stature. Virginia sent Washington, Wythe, Mason (who refused to sign) and Madison (then an unknown factor). It did not send Jefferson, Marshall, Monroe, Patrick Henry, any of the Lees, or numerous others entitled to rank as Founders if not Framers. Indeed, Virginia could have found several dozen men equal or superior to McClung or Blair or Edmund Randolph.

The glorification of the Framers as demigods is a form of mystification that naturally lends itself to elitist rule. If the Constitution is a miracle, then it has to be treated as a holy object and handled only by the priests, not by the common run of humanity. To treat the Philadelphia Convention as a gathering of demigods is worse than foolish and undemocratic; it prevents any real appreciation of their achievement.

The members of the Convention, the Framers, were an able lot; some were great. Yet, in the final analysis, they were not omnipotent or omniscient but merely the delegates of the States. Some very able men who were selected by the States refused to go, either because they had more pressing business or were suspicious of the proceedings. Others were quite desultory in attendance, and several of the best men there refused to sign the finished product.

Nor did the Framers establish or proclaim a new Constitution, something they had no authority to do. What they did was draw up a convincing and appealing proposal—convincing and appealing because it tended to meet the occasion and to anticipate the future—a proposal that, after a considerable amount of explanation and qualification and amendments promised, was approved eventually by an effective majority of the people in each of the States—that is, by the people of the United States as already defined by existing political communities. Those who ratified the Constitution are its real Founders (as opposed to its Framers). It is wrong, therefore, to cite the debates in Philadelphia as definitive of "original intent," as useful and illuminating as they may be in a subsidiary sense. It is the powers that ratified it that determine, in the final analysis, what the "intention" of the Constitution is. Madison himself stated this truth. Fortunately, to declare this is merely to declare the validity of democracy and of federalism.

How far we fall short of their achievement. In truth, in the Framers' Constitution, one of the things they took for granted (that we have lost) was an adequate supply of intelligence and honour. At the time of the Framers the justices of the peace of any small county in Virginia or the selectmen of any town in Connecticut could have mustered more intelligence (I leave aside less measurable virtues) than the whole of the government today.

By intelligence I mean learning, wisdom, foresight, digested experience, detachment, ethics. Not shrewdness in self-promotion, conceit, visionary schemes, and vague good intentions. The Founding Fathers did not anticipate the ravages of the two-party system and its ability to foist cunning mediocrities on the public, The Constitution presupposed an inexhaustible supply of able and honourable and *independent* public men (whose ambitions needed to be watched). Almost all of our leaders are now the creatures of political parties, which means that they are more adept at winning offices than at filling them, at conniving and self-promotion than at statesmanship.

The replacement of the independent gentleman by the professional politician beginning in the 19th century, a reflection of changes in society and of the capacity of clever men to manipulate even wisely constructed institutions to their advantage, provided as serious a distortion of the Constitution as did the concomitant rise of lawyers. It would astound our politicians today to learn that at the time of the Founders and even long after, people held public office for duty and honour and that in most cases, rather than filling their own snouts at the public trough (except for a few bond speculators), they actually made a sacrifice of their private interests to serve in public office. The Constitution presupposed an aristocratic rather than a professional class of office holders and aspirants as members of Congress and Presidential Electors, who would always be capable of independent judgment. That is, the operation of the Constitution rested in part on something that has ceased to exist.

The essence of republican government was that the will of the people prevailed but that it was formulated by able and independent delegates. When we say the will of the people, we have to avoid the mystical and high-flying references to something strongly akin to the General Will, which we all know is not the will of the people but the will of the vanguard of the proletariat on behalf of the people—what the people would want if they were as smart and virtuous as their masters. This too easily merges over into "all mankind," so that everyone in the world becomes by extension an American citizen—something which if taken literally constitutes a grave threat both to the United States and to mankind. The will of the people under the Constitution can only mean the deliberate sense of the political communities, that is the States, that *are* the United States, expressed through the republican mechanisms that are established. This suggests that judicial review must be relegated to a subsidiary role.

Original intent, properly speaking, is a legal and not a constitutional idea. The original intent of a piece of legislation may be juridically determined by reference to its legislative history (though given the trickery and evasiveness of recent Congresses this is not as simple as it might be). However, "original intent" of the Constitution is not similarly determinable by judges because the intent was given to the Constitution by the people who ratified it. An appeal to the Philadelphia convention, known chiefly through the partial notes of Madison, is not strictly analogous to an appeal to legislative history. The Constitution can be interpreted finally only historically, not juridically. It is also important to note that the "original intent" of a particular provision of the Constitution and the "original intent" of the Constitution in the large sense are different questions.

Clyde N. Wilson

I have often heard members of Congress and other public officers answer a constitutional question with the quip that they are not constitutional lawyers. Nonsense! Members of Congress, the President, and more importantly, the people and officials of the States have just as much standing in interpreting the Constitution as any panel of lawyers or law professors, whether or not the latter have yet been appointed to the federal bench. The Founders never intended that the high *political* questions of constitutional interpretation would be at the mercy of lawyers' tricks.

The Federalist justices of the early 19th century—Marshall, Story, etc.— were legalists and devotees of the British Common Law. In one of the most misguided feats in American history, they infused judicial review into the constitutional process, believing they were providing a check to unruly popular passions and lending stability to the institutions of self-government. But while they did inject a type of stability, their efforts had a pragmatic and centralising tendency that carried the emphasis away from the historical rights of the States and from the consent of the people. It is not difficult to understand why Jefferson feared the judiciary as the greatest of all enemies of republican government.

There is a piece of erroneous folklore, a 19th century distortion of the Founding, that the Constitution is in the special keeping of lawyers. In fact, relatively few of the Framers were practicing lawyers. Primarily they occupied their time as owners of plantations or other large estates or as merchants (that is, not counter-jumpers but traders on a large scale). They were also clergymen and educators, among other represented professions. It is true that a good many were trained in law. Law was considered a useful study which enhanced one's ability to manage one's own interests and participate in public life because it was a storehouse of English traditions of order and liberty. However, it was not considered, except by a few of the Framers who were not the most trustworthy, that a primary attention to the daily practice of law was the best role for a statesman.

The Founders recognised no aristocracies except those of talent, service, and social weight. They would regard the Constitution today as captive to an oligarchy of federal judges, drawn from a class of lawyers and law professors whose study is not of noble traditions of liberty and order but of the defense of

40

large vested interests, whether of big business or the established left-wing causes. It would be difficult to imagine any group, taken as a group, more dissimilar to the great landowners and republican gentlemen of the Founding than the choice legal scholars of today's America. The former were representatives of their communities and the bearers of wisdom and vision, the latter are the representatives of vested interests and the perpetrators of arcane manipulations.

We have here more than the elitist tendencies of 20th-century liberalism or "guardian democracy." We are going to have to go back a lot further than the Warren Court or the New Deal to remedy the ill. An evolutionary captivity of the Constitution was inevitable once the Constitution was given over largely into the hands of lawyers and treated primarily as a legal document, the understanding of which was to rest on the reasoning of judges.

This is a major problem that the Framers, for the most part, did not expect. The Constitution was not intended to be, except in a subsidiary sense, a legal document. It was not expected that it would be interpreted by lawyers (people who argue cases for pay) much less by law professors (people who teach others how to argue for pay). The Constitution is a political document. Lawyers and judges are qualified to deal with legal matters. Study of the law per se, or pursuance of legal procedures per se, will never yield an accurate or lasting interpretation of the Constitution in the large sense. Note that the speeches and documents of the early national period, like the Virginia and Kentucky Resolutions, treat Constitutional understanding as a high political matter. But through the 14th Amendment and the usurpations of all three branches of the federal government, every conceivable legal question has also been made into a *constitutional* question. And even if this process yields a workable rendering of particular clauses of the Constitution, it should not be allowed cumulatively to determine the meaning of the Constitution itself.

We know that the Constitution has changed and continues to do so. If we look into what Constitution deserves our respect, we find two current views. One view, put forth by recent Supreme Courts and their defenders, says that the Constitution is an evolutionary document whose great virtue lies in its adaptability. According to this, it follows that it is the right or even the duty of the Supreme Court from time to time to bring the Constitution "up to date" with "modern" sensibilities. We can hardly deny that the Constitution has changed and evolved. It has a history. However, from the observation that the Constitution must be viewed historically, it does not necessarily follow that the Supreme Court should be the arbiter of direction. In fact, this would not have been accepted by the main body of Founders.

The other view of the Constitution current today is that we are bound by its "intent." The Founders, at least that majority who were not over-involved in a specific agenda, would not have demurred from this proposition. But is it not obviously true that *the intent of the Constitution* is *a historical question?* That is to say, questions of "original intent" are most properly answered, not by legal reasoning and legal tradition, nor by abstract speculation on democratic philosophy or individual "rights," but by reference to the historical record. In emphasizing the historical record there are two things I am not saying. I am not suggesting, in the manner of Charles Beard, that there is some secret dirty story to be ferreted out by historians. Nor am I saying that only professional historians can be allowed to put the Constitution in context, for any intelligent person may make a valid historical observation.

If we do not rely on the stream of legal interpretation to discern the intent of the Constitution nor on the specialist knowledge of historians, nor on philosophical speculation (however relevant any of these may be in a subordinate sense), what do we rely on? We rely on history, and history, if it is not a specialist's but a people's history, is exactly what we mean by tradition. After all, the Constitution rests upon the consent of the people. And it is therefore, in the final analysis, the people who have a right to determine its intent. If we argue that this is a perilous or unworkable doctrine, then we are merely declaring that democracy and federalism are unacceptable.

Of course, if we accept this proposition, our problems are only beginning, for we are still faced with the task of translating the people's right to interpret their Constitution into established mechanisms of government. Most of those who think of themselves as "conservatives" through the 20th century, relied on appointing Supreme Court justices who are devoted to "original intent." Such a strategy has been a catastrophic failure. The people must begin to look into our tradition for other remedies, among which State interposition is one.

THE REVOLUTION AS SECESSION

A SUCCESSFUL WAR of Independence established thirteen free and independent States in North America in 1783. This was followed, unfortunately for us, by the French Revolution and then by the 19th century, pre-eminently a time of violent government centralisation. Subsequent events, as well as nationalistic emotion and propaganda, have seriously damaged our ability to see what the American Revolution meant to the people who carried it out.

From the founding of Jamestown in 1607 to the outbreak of hostilities in 1775 is 168 years. In that long period each colony developed its own society. They shared Christianity and an inheritance of English law, but also had a consciousness of their differences in interests and values. An imperial threat to their well-established tradition of virtual self-government brought them all, finally, to resist an attempted increment of British power over their internal affairs—the American Revolution. It was, as the great M.E. Bradford observed, not a revolution made but a revolution averted—a counter-revolution to preserve their existing societies.

Anyone who reads the debates on the ratification of the U.S. Constitution will see that its purpose was the same, the preservation of the existing societies. This was true for most, although there were centralist rent-seekers lurking on the margins whose dubiously constitutional agenda came forward as soon as the federal government got under way. For most an alliance to institutionalise cooperation in certain common concerns of the free and independent States seemed to be called for, although giving more power to a central authority presented potential dangers that should be guarded against. That was the purpose of the first Ten Amendments, subsequently known as the Bill of Rights. Americans had a considerable degree of patriotic fellow feeling but their association was not a nation but a confederacy. And the best of them feared what they called "consolidation"—too much power at the center.

Here are a couple of simple truths, unknown to Presidents and Supreme Court justices. Before the War between the States "United States" was always a plural in every legal document and public discussion. The United States "are,"

43

not the United States "is," was the universal usage, as in the Constitution itself. Second, nobody today ever calls the Constitution by its correct name, which is, as it says, "a Constitution FOR the United States." Not "the U.S. Constitution" or "the Constitution OF the U.S.," but a Constitution FOR the States United.

Let us see how this conception of the American Union was alive well into the 19th century heyday of centralised and supreme government.

Thomas Jefferson was an American patriot. He was not a nationalist advocate of "one nation indivisible." During and after his time nationalism was becoming a dominant force in the Western world, including the plural United States. Nationalism meant a territory politically and economically controlled by a central state and an emotional attachment to that state. For Jefferson as for nearly all the Founders, one could be an American patriot without requiring unreserved obedience to the central government or believing that the people and their freedoms were spiritually inseparable from that government.

American nationalists glory in imagining Jefferson, having consummated the Louisiana Purchase, sitting in the presidential mansion celebrating the growing power and glory of the mighty new nation, the United States. Not a bit of it. This picture is an invention of the imperialist later 19th century. At the time, Jefferson writes to a close associate:

> The future inhabitants of the Atlantic and Mississippi States will be our sons. We leave them in distinct but bordering establishments. We think we see their happiness in their Union, and we wish it. Events may prove otherwise; and if they see their interest in separation, why should we take side with our Atlantic rather than our Mississippi descendants? It is but the elder and the younger son differing. God bless them both, and keep them in union, if it be for their good, but separate them, if it be better.

A letter to the English savant Joseph Priestly about the same time carries the same idea. After expressing relief that the worrisome problem of a Napoleonic empire on the Mississippi has been solved, Jefferson writes:

> The *denouement* has been very happy; and I confess I look to this duplication for the extending a government so free and economical as

ours, as a great achievement to the mass of happiness that is to ensue. Whether we remain in one confederacy, or form into Atlantic and Mississippi confederacies, I believe not very important to the happiness of either part. Those of the western confederacy will be as much our children and descendants as those of the eastern.

Note that Mr. Jefferson envisioned a future of self-governing commonwealths made up of the descendants of Americans, not a global melting pot. And the new societies to the West would be created by the people, not by the federal government. The Union was not sacred and eternal. It was an arrangement that could be changed. What was important was the principle of self-government. He firmly opposed the Northern effort in Congress to dictate the constitution of the sovereign people of Missouri on the pretence of antislavery, and in the last months of his life he wrote that it would be better for Virginia to secede than to succumb to the centralisation pushed by Northern rent-seekers under John Quincy Adams.

The Jeffersonian conception of a Union founded as a disposable alliance lasted a long time. In the 1830s the famed observer Alexis de Tocqueville wrote in *Democracy in America:*

The Union was formed by the voluntary agreement of the States; and these, in uniting together, have not forfeited their sovereignty, nor have they been reduced to the condition of one and the same people. If one of the States chose to withdraw its name from the contract, it would be difficult to disprove its right of doing so . . . .

And the New Yorker and American patriot James Fenimore Cooper in *The American Democrat* (1838) writes that the Union is "a compact between separate communities." "The union of these States is founded on an express compromise . . . . And it is not its intention to reach a benefit, however considerable, by extorting undue sacrifices from particular members of the Confederacy." This last is a remark against the Whig tariff which profited wealthy Northerners at the expense of the South. He is suggesting that the South might justly consider such to be a violation of the compact.

In 1863 Abraham Lincoln declared in pseudo-Biblical language that our forefathers had brought forth "a new nation, conceived in liberty and dedicated to the proposition that all men are created" and that "we are engaged in a great civil war testing whether that nation or any nation so conceived and so dedicated can long endure." Lincoln at Gettysburg committed a quadruple lie that has since become standard American doctrine about the Revolution. First, what was created in 1776 was not a nation but an alliance. At that time there was not even the Articles of Confederation. Second, he elevated the bit of *obiter dicta* about equality above the Declaration's fundamental assertion of the right of societies of men to govern themselves by their own lights, attaching a phony moralistic motive to the invasion and conquest of the South—what Bradford called "the rhetoric of continuing revolution." Third, Lincoln was not engaged in preserving the Union. The Union was destroyed the moment he had undertaken to overthrow the legitimate governments of 15 States by force. He was establishing the supremacy of the government machinery in Washington which he controlled over the many self-governing communities of Americans. Fourth, he cast the Revolution in a mystical way, as if the forefathers had met on Mount Olympus and decreed liberty. But governments, even of the wisest men, cannot decree liberty. The Revolutionary Americans were fighting to preserve the liberty they already had through their history, which many saw as a benevolent gift of Providence.

Did not Jefferson Davis have a better grasp of the Revolution when he said that Southerners were simply imitating their forebears and that the Confederacy "illustrates the American idea that government rests upon the consent of the governed"?

The desire for "consolidation" on the part of some Americans, perhaps not a majority, had reached with Lincoln the point that the observations made by Tocqueville and Cooper were no longer relevant. Clearly, the government, the machinery controlled by the politicians in Washington, who had been chosen by 2/5ths of the people, now had supremacy over the life and institutions of Americans.

A half century later, Theodore Roosevelt invoked the Louisiana Purchase and the Monroe Doctrine as Jeffersonian precedents for imperialism. In my invariably humble opinion, Mr. Jefferson (and Washington too) would not be pleased to become an icon on Mount Rushmore along with the blood and iron nationalists Lincoln and Roosevelt. Jefferson's vision of peopling the North American continent with American farmers is something very different from Northern capitalists using the armed forces to seize Cuba and the Philippines. When Jefferson looked westward he saw succeeding generations of Americans creating new self-governing commonwealths joined in such confederacies as they wished. Lincoln's Republican defenders of "the Union" saw something very different when they looked in that direction. They saw natural resources to be exploited, new markets to be developed behind a tariff wall that diverted wealth to favoured Northern interests, more political offices to be filled by their party, more immigrants to be lured, which would keep down the wages of native labour and enhance the value of the lands to be given to corporations by the government. That is what they meant by "preserving the Union." The "one nation indivisible," now as well as then is a tool of powerful interests, not a sacred bond of patriots.

Let's compare Lincoln's version of the Founding with John C. Calhoun's, delivered in 1841. Calhoun points out that Providence had made ideal conditions for the development of American liberty. The resistance of the Indians and the settling of a wilderness were challenging enough to require "hardy and enterprising emigrants," but not harsh enough to require the power of centralised government. "It is to settlements formed by individuals so influenced, and thrown, from the beginning, on their own resources, almost exclusively, that we owe our enterprise, energy, love of liberty, and capacity for self-government. "No Olympian wisdom at the center decreed American liberty.

As you will recall, Carolina began as a grant by Charles II to eight Lords Proprietors. In 1720 the South Carolina colonists had just fought a bloody Indian war and found that the agents of the Proprietors were intent on engrossing for themselves the lands that had been cleared as a result. The elected assembly and the militia, reflecting the consensus of South Carolina society, simply refused to obey the legal but foreign authority and effectively terminated the Proprietors' power. That was 1720, a half century before the Revolution.

Before the joint Declaration of Independence, the South Carolinians were already independent. They alone defeated a large British fleet trying to capture Charleston. The city did not fall until it was surrendered by a Yankee general sent by the Continental Congress.

Resistance continued under the partisan bands of Francis Marion, Thomas Sumter, and Andrew Pickens. These were all volunteers fighting to defend their state, irregulars not eligible for the pensions that Massachusetts men later lined up for more numerously than had ever seen active service. This was all done without the least participation by any central government power. It was this resistance, along with Southern Continental regiments, that led to Guilford Courthouse and Yorktown and forced the British to give up.

I would note that real societies produce real leaders—farseeing statesmen who serve their people. Think of the incredible supply of world-class leadership produced by the American Revolution. But centralised power can only produce politicians—ambitious and conniving people contending for possession of the government machinery that conveys them benefits.

The struggle for Independence produced leaders willing to sacrifice for the liberty of their people. All Patriots were threatened by and many suffered the loss of property. The pledge of "lives, fortunes, and sacred honour" was very real. Two of South Carolina's Signers of the Declaration were imprisoned in a vile British fort in St. Augustine, another leader in the Tower of London. Governor John Rutledge spent much of the war as a fugitive on horseback. He did not need a capitol building and a bureaucracy to make his writ run because he was the acknowledged leader of a people. The same was true later of the governors of several occupied Confederate states. Communities in the Upcountry were massacred by Tories and Indians.

South Carolina acted in 1720 as a sovereign society. It acted exactly the same when it declared and fought for independence from Britain, when it ratified the U.S. Constitution, when it nullified the Tariff of Abominations in 1832, and when it dissolved its ties with the Union in 1860. All of these matters were hotly debated and when the decision was taken the people rallied around to defend their Society. Centralised governments like the U.S. do not have debate and deliberation to establish what is best. They merely have verbal stunts among those contending for power.

In the last months of his life, South Carolina's greatest son, Calhoun, worked on a final bequest, his treatise "A Disquisition on Government." Calhoun's immediate family history included the settlement of the upcountry by those "hardy and enterprising immigrants" who created their own economy, justice, religious institutions, and self-defense without reference to any outside and superior government power. Calhoun likewise was familiar with the Revolution, the ratification of the Constitution, and the South Carolina constitution of 1810 which created a workable compromise between the differing societies of the Low Country and Up Country. There were no remote "forefathers" here. It was the experience of his own father.

He begins his "Disquisition" by discarding the notion of all men being born free and equal, not because he wants to defend slavery but because he wants us to begin in the right place. All of us are born as helpless babes who cannot survive a day without society. God has created man a social animal. He needs society to survive, much less to realise his highest potential. Societies are a given, created by history and human nature. But men have selfish as well as social feelings, which demands inevitably a government of some kind to keep the peace and enforce justice. While society is created by God, governments are only creations of men, existing for the protection of society. And since those entrusted with government have selfish feelings like all other men, a good government will have a constitution, not so much a grant of power as a statement of the limits of power.

I want us to think of the order of precedence Calhoun established. Society, which is ordained by God for our benefit, comes first. It is pre-existent. Government, created only by men, is something distinct that rightly exists solely for the protection of society. Further, a Constitution in its true sense is that by which society limits and restrains those who are entrusted with government. It is not an open-ended charter of their powers. When a government is unrestrained, there is no Constitution, by whatever name called. Today real restraint on the federal government does not exist. But we have a Bill of Rights, intended to limit the federal government's depredations on the communities of men, turned on its head to authorise the federal government to reconstruct society according to the whims of the Bankers, Bombers, and Busy-Bodies who govern us.

The American consolidated government rests on two pillars. The first is economic. A huge area concentrated as one market has a broad appeal and can be pictured as patriotic and a necessity for prosperity. Of course, rent-seekers and ambitious politicians find central power much easier to control than diverse and dispersed authority, as well as providing a much larger field of loot. That is why we find Hamilton disregarding the Constitution that had just been ratified and at the first opportunity paying off the inflated war debt at face value with interest-bearing federal bonds and setting up a private banking cartel with the profitable privilege of controlling the currency. Jeffersonians denounced this as a "paper aristocracy" and a betrayal of the Revolution. Through the early 19th century they were able to hold the line against the rent-seekers' complete control of the federal government. With the Lincoln revolution the Hamiltonian program triumphed. Indeed, that was the purpose of the Lincoln revolution. Thus today, all the politicians of both parties rally around so that the taxpayers and posterity can reward the Banksters, Too Big to Jail, for their evil deeds.

The second pillar of nationalism is emotional. Patriots love and are willing to defend their people and that portion of earth which their people inhabit. Nationalists progressively fail to understand a distinction between the society, and the government machinery. Urban populations without any real religion or culture, like much of the U.S. today, cling to government as the source of identity and the meaning of their existence. Whenever I criticize the federal government I get emails threatening to kill me just like my treasonous Southern ancestors. I can make a whole book of the fulminations these numerous proto-fascist American patriots. I submit that Americans properly swear allegiance to the Constitution, not to the government or its banner.

Nationalism is inevitably imperialistic. It fosters competition between powerful governments. An end result was the still incredible bloodletting of World War I. You would think that would have cured people of nationalism. If not that, you would think the craziness would have finally died with Hitler's legions in the snows of Russia. But, alas, it remains very much alive in the ruling class of the U.S.A. During the Cold War, we know that the CIA had a plan to kill Americans and blame it on Castro. America is not a value to these people, not a living thing to be preserved. It is merely the power base from which they play games with the masters of other power bases.

President George W. Bush stated that it was the goal of America to rid the world of evil. Yes, he actually said that. And note that ridding the world of evil he sees not as a crusade, or a mission, or a duty, but a goal, like in sports or salesmanship. If we were not used to this kind of rhetoric and did not already know that the speaker is a simpleton, we would have to judge him to be a lunatic. American citizens, it would seem, are not to go about their business— doing useful work, taking care of their families and friends, dealing justly and charitably with their neighbours, keeping the peace, and seeking their eternal salvation as best they can. They are merely the expendable raw material of an insane government project. It is then perfectly good for the government to elect a new people as it is now doing with immigration. The government is sacred and eternal and may do with the society whatever those who control its power can imagine. All that is good and noble in the American Revolution's establishment of self-government has been reversed to servitude. A perverted Bill of Rights has been one of the sharpest weapons of the tyrant.

DEVOLUTION

Preface to *Confederates in the Boardroom: The New Science of Organisations*
by Michael Tuggle

EQUIPPED WITH AN ABUNDANT knowledge of history, Michael Tuggle has cast a discerning eye on the trends of the present. Not the 'trendy' trends but the real ones, those which can guide our steps into the future (as far as the future can be known to us mortals). The trends suggest to him something very hopeful—the probability and suitability of a change in the principle by which human affairs are governed. We have been living for a long time by the organizing principle of command from the top down—something the American Founding Fathers decried as "consolidation"—and the opposite of liberty.

Throughout most of the course of Western Civilisation, until a little over two centuries ago, centralised government was regarded as something bad and alien, characteristic of "Oriental despotism." The Greeks, for example, were divided into self-governing city-states. They were never united under one authority during the time when their excellence in knowledge, art, and government reached levels that still astonish the world. Herodotus, the first historian, ascribed the Greeks' defeat of the Persian Empire to the resilience flowing from their freedom from arbitrary control. In typical fashion, government-worshipping historians of the nineteenth century forward preached the contrary: that the decline of the ancient Greeks resulted from their lack of unity.

However, a more reasonable interpretation is that, although they were damaged by fighting among themselves, the Greeks met with irredeemable disaster only after Athens and Sparta had centralised a dangerous power to dictate to the other city-states. Thus, the Greeks' liberties and creativity ended precisely when they were united under the Macedonian monarchy.

John C. Calhoun, one of the great anti-consolidationist thinkers of the nineteenth century, pointed out that the Romans achieved their greatest freedom and strength as a people when there existed two centers of power—the

Senate and the Tribunes—each with a veto over the other's actions. The workings of the state required co-ordination and agreement among the elements of society rather than dictation from above. Contrary to government-worshippers who complained that the lack of a commanding central authority made society helpless, Calhoun observed that an independent consensus of the parts led to actions that were highly effective and more satisfactory to the whole. No central authority could match the strength of free men who co-operated willingly. Mr. Tuggle enlightens us as to the current appropriateness of Calhoun's insight.

Even under the Roman Empire (while it was healthy), although policies were sent out from the center, vast areas of initiative remained in the provinces and cities—in military affairs, taxation, local government, and religion.

The Middle Ages were par excellence the age of decentralisation; there was scarcely any real power that was not local. Kings and lesser lords essentially depended upon the voluntary co-operation of their vassals. The Church, at least in appearance, was centralised in its own affairs, but it preached the rightness of subsidiarity in government. Our modern thinkers who extol the necessity and glory of the nation-state consolidated under one supreme authority tell us that decentralisation was the cause of the "darkness" of those times. Looked at another way, perhaps it was the creative force of many different points of light that illuminated the way of the West out of the darkness—a darkness brought on by the inevitable collapse of the muscle-bound inflexibility of the Roman imperial government. Certainly, the lights came on earliest in the free and self-governing cities, while the Renaissance blazed most brightly in the free and independent cities of northern Italy—not in some large centrally-managed country

In the seventeenth century it was thought that the 'Sun King' of France, Louis XIV, had brought centralised government to the height of its possibilities. Louis could oppress individuals; however, he could not—except through the traditional hodgepodge of taxes—oppress entire classes. He could declare wars, but he could no more command all the manpower and resources of the kingdom for his wars than he could the rotation of the planets. It was his nationalist successors of the Revolution and the Empire who marshaled the ability of a centralised government to command a whole society. Their handiwork was copied all over the Western world. The consolidated nation-state became the material and psychological focus of entire peoples while the ensuing conflicts among such states became the prevailing pattern of history. The American Revolution—and the Articles of Confederation and Constitution which followed—preceded the triumph of the nation-state. During the long colonial period, Americans enjoyed the benign neglect of the British Crown. The thirteen colonies barely felt the hand of central government (their citizens scarcely feeling the controlling hand of any government). It was the British government's attempt to end this happy condition that brought them to declare that the thirteen "are and ought to be free and independent States."

The American Founders intended to create a Union which would institutionalise bonds of co-operation among those states and among the new commonwealths that their descendants would create out of wilderness in the future. They did not intend to establish a central authority, such as the one they had just thrown off, from which there was no escape or appeal except by the sword. They dreaded the specter of "consolidation" which, if allowed, would bring an end to their individual freedom and the self-government of their natural communities. Human associations in community were distinct from and took precedence over governments. Good governments were the servants of society, not its master.

The forces that reshaped the States United into the United State in the middle of the nineteenth century did so only as the result of the destruction of the essential elements of self-government and a holocaust of American lives.

The supposed deep thinkers of the nineteenth century (especially in Germany and the United States) celebrated the brutality employed against their fellow countrymen that was necessary in order to establish the nation-states they desired. Each sang the praises of his own country's new ability to mobilise the property and allegiance of the masses to the ends of the central state. Nationalist mania stipulated that the centralised state was a prerequisite for the liberation and progress of humanity.

Lord Acton, an immensely learned historian of liberty, was, like Calhoun, a naysayer of the nineteenth century, bringing into common reference the phrase

"Power corrupts." The progress of man depended upon ordered liberty; and liberty depended upon the restraint and dispersal of power. Acton demonstrated that freedom in the Western world was a product of restrictions on power that had been painfully accumulated bit by bit over the course of centuries. Taking the long view, Acton wrote, the crushing of the principle of states' rights in the American war of 1861--1865 was not a victory for liberty but a defeat.

One wonders why in the twenty-first century anyone of good faith should continue to give devotion to the principle of consolidation. The postulate of the all-commanding central government has resulted, for the first time in mankind's long and painful existence, in what were literally World Wars. The central state has given rulers the power to murder the innocents of their own and other countries by the millions. Even at its least destructive, the central state inevitably, as Calhoun also observed, preys upon the people, or a part of them, for the benefit of those who hold power and their clients.

Surely the premier empirical truth that emerged from human affairs in the twentieth century is that free markets are better than central planning. At least better for society as a whole, aside from those who profit from the Plan. As Tuggle makes clear, confidence in the necessity of centralised power in industrial management, education, and the organisation of many other human affairs has proved to be a delusion over the past two centuries. The wisdom of experience and of insight into the real trends of the present which the author has brought to bear tell us that centralisation has not fulfilled the promises of its apologists. Command from the top down has proven itself to be not only arbitrary and inimical to freedom, but also inefficient and unable to adapt to changing circumstances.

The wave of the future, the cutting edge, the hope of efficiency, abundance, and freedom for societies is just what the Western tradition has always told us—devolution of power to competing and co-operating authorities. There is no lesson that it is more important to take to heart at this moment in time. It seems that John C. Calhoun was right after all.

Q & A ON NULLIFICATION AND INTERPOSITION

Q: WHAT CAN I READ that can give me a serious overview of the true impact of the tariffs of 1828 and 1832 on South Carolina?

A: I think the question of the impact of the protective tariff on South Carolina is the wrong question to ask. It is something of a diversionary tactic, for reasons I will try to explain below.

The questions to ask about that period of American history are

1. Was the protective tariff just?
2. Was it good policy?
3. Was it constitutional?

A believer in free markets and constitutionally limited government can only give a resounding NO to all these questions.

It was not just South Carolina that objected to the tariff. From the earliest national period John Taylor's writings and John Randolph's speeches, along with many other Southern spokesmen, were eloquent and firm on the unjustness of the "protective" tariff. From 1824 on, every Southern legislature strongly condemned the tariff. The difference was that only South Carolina was willing to go to the extent of actual nullification. This was not because South Carolina had suffered any more than others, but because South Carolina was the only State in which decisions could be made without the input of national party leaders who wanted to obfuscate and avoid hard issues.

From 1824 on it was apparent that the manufacturers intended a high and permanent system of tariffs, which had not been obvious before, when tariffs had been thought of as revenue measures with perhaps "incidental" protection. The term "lobbyists" was first used in America in the 1820s for the agents of the New England/Pennsylvania manufacturers who began to haunt the legislative halls and hold out inducements to congressmen. The acts of 1828 and 1832 were blatant examples of log-rolling rather than policy decisions. The latter was also deceptively presented by the Jackson/Van Buren forces as a remedy of tariff abuses.

It was not only the South that vigorously opposed the tariffs of 1828 and 1832. Northern free market men like William Gouge and Condy Raguet exposed the tariff and approved South Carolina's action, and public meetings of Northern merchants and craftsmen denounced the protective tariff as did Democratic conventions in many Northern States at that time and later.

Historians have tried with considerable success to divert the question to an emphasis on South Carolina. The hidden assumption is that the tariff policy is so self-evidently good that there is something peculiar about South Carolina to explain the strong opposition. It must be exhausted soil and declining prosperity (or more recently fears over slavery) that drove South Carolinians to blame their problems on others. This is just a transmission of the claims of the tariffites' propaganda of the time. New Englanders, then as now, were extremely self-centered and self-righteous. They said in Congress that the South's economic problems were because Southerners were, unlike them, lazy and unproductive. (Calhoun pointed out that Southerners produced almost all of the country's foreign trade to be sold in an open market while those who complained of Southern lack of enterprise enjoyed a protected domestic market.) Many New England spokesmen said that opposition to such a self-evidently good policy was itself treason. Not nullification, mind you, but opposition to the protective tariff—that is, opposing the demands of New England—was in itself declared to be treasonous. The historians who concentrate on "the effects on South Carolina" work from a basic assumption that Southerners are too stupid to know their own real interests, are always wrong and deceptive in their politics, and are naturally inclined to be traitors.

So, to approach the question of the tariff as an issue of the peculiarities of South Carolina is a diversion from the larger question of the impact of the tariff on the American economy as a whole. How can any free marketeer doubt that the effect was unjust? Even more so because it not only benefited one group of people, but it also, on phony grounds of patriotism, diverted wealth from the South to certain interests in the North in a government that was supposed to benefit all parts of the Union. It was this (far more than the slavery issue) that drove Southerners to begin to question the value of the Union. Was the North to get all the benefits and the South to bear all the burdens?

What was the impact of the tariffs on South Carolina? This is an empirical question that, as in any complicated situation, can be argued all sorts of ways. It would seem to be axiomatic to advocates of free markets that a government policy that artificially raises the costs of goods for the benefit of a particular interest is harmful. But in a sense that is beside the point. What was the economic effect of the Tea Tax on the American colonists in 1775? The point was that it was an unfair imposition based on an exercise of doubted power.

You can get a good overview of the Southern case from the section on Free Trade in my *The Essential Calhoun*, especially Calhoun's speech on the tariff of 1842. Also my article on Calhoun and Free Trade in the Genovese festschrift, *Slavery, Secession, and Southern History*, edited by Robert Paquette.

Q: How about the constitutional question—is there really no good constitutional argument on behalf of tariffs for protection?

A: There is no question that the Constitution gave certain taxing powers for the purpose of providing the general government with a source of support. The tax on imports was the best way to do this. It was paid by the consumer to the degree of consumption of imported goods, largely luxury items or highly specialized materials and equipment. Equally there is no question that a protective tariff is anti-revenue—using a law for a different purpose than that for which the power had been granted. The Supreme Court held that it was a political question, that it could not look beneath the law itself to its intentions or effects. In the Philadelphia Convention, proposals that the new federal government have the power to lay protective tariffs and to charter corporations failed to carry. As Tom DiLorenzo has recently reminded us, the Hamiltonians cavalierly disregarded the limits on federal power in both these cases in pursuit of their mercantilist, mimic England, agenda. It is perhaps also worth pointing out in this connection that the Constitution absolutely forbade any tax on exports.

Nullification

Q: And finally, do you believe nullification would have to involve convening a special convention of the people, or could it conceivably be carried out by a state legislature?

A: The South Carolina nullification of 1832 was enacted by a convention of the people especially called for the purpose. By the South Carolina constitution such a convention could only be called by a three/fourths majority of both houses of the legislature. The South Carolinians wanted to make it clear that the act was a high constitutional one—based on the primary sovereignty of the people—like the acts that had made the State independent in 1775 and had ratified the Constitution in 1788. However, the Kentucky and Virginia Resolutions of 1798 and 1799, which laid out the power and right of state interposition against unconstitutional federal acts, were done by the legislatures. But they were statements of intent to nullify rather than acts of nullification.

A couple more points. "Nullification" was a derogatory, negative-sounding term invented by the opponents of the right. The proper name is State Interposition.

The historians tell us that Nullification of the tariff by South Carolina failed and federal supremacy was vindicated. That is not quite the whole truth. One can make a good case that it was a success. The historians note Jackson's proclamation against nullification but they never mention that there was a great outpouring of public opinion against Jackson's proclamation. The proclamation raised the possibility of the coercion of the people of a State by the federal government. Many people, North and South, were more alarmed by that than they were disturbed by nullification. (By the way, Webster DID NOT win the Webster-Hayne Debate. In the Senate, the press, and public opinion, Webster was the clear loser.)

Nullification was a success. To defuse the crisis, Congress in 1833 passed the Compromise Tariff by which the tariff would come down by stages over the next ten years, after which it would be at a revenue-only. Not bad for a small State against the world. True, the Whigs sought to forget and violate the compromise in 1842, but they did not entirely succeed and the most free-trade tariff in our history was passed in 1846. This would not have happened if it had not been for the action of "our gallant little State."

Q: What is the proper reply to the States which, objecting to the Virginia and Kentucky Resolutions, cited Article III, Section 2 as evidence that the Supreme Court is indeed the arbiter for disputes of power between the federal government and the states?

A: The States that took the position you cite were those deeply invested in Federalist hegemony—devoted to constructing a strong federal judiciary to control what they regarded as the evil and unenlightened masses. They said so very plainly. Was not this position thoroughly repudiated in the Kentucky and Virginia documents themselves, followed immediately by the triumph of the "Principles of 1798" party in the elections? Where does it say that the Supreme Court and not the people have the final say on interpretation?

ABOUT THE AUTHOR

DR. CLYDE WILSON is Emeritus Distinguished Professor of History of the University of South Carolina, where he served from 1971 to 2006. He holds a Ph.D. from the University of North Carolina at Chapel Hill. He recently completed editing of a 28-volume edition of *The Papers of John C. Calhoun* which has received high praise for quality. He is author or editor of more than a dozen other books and over 600 articles, essays, and reviews in a variety of books and journals, and has lectured all over the U.S. and in Europe, many of his lectures having been recorded online and on CDs and DVDs. Dr. Wilson directed 17 doctoral dissertations, a number of which have been published. Books written or edited include *Why the South Will Survive, Carolina Cavalier: The Life and Mind of James Johnston Pettigrew, The Essential Calhoun,* three volumes of *The Dictionary of Literary Biography* on American Historians, *From Union to Empire: Essays in the Jeffersonian Tradition, Defending Dixie: Essays in Southern History and Culture, Chronicles of the South* and *The Yankee Problem.* Dr. Wilson is founding director of the Society of Independent Southern Historians; former president of the St. George Tucker Society for Southern Studies; recipient of the Bostick Prize for Contributions to South Carolina Letters, of the first annual John Randolph Society Lifetime Achievement Award, and of the Robert E. Lee Medal of the Sons of Confederate Veterans. He is M.E. Bradford Distinguished Professor of the Abbeville Institute; Contributing Editor of *Chronicles: A Magazine of American Culture;* founding dean of the Stephen D. Lee Institute, educational arm of the Sons of Confederate Veterans; and co-founder of Shotwell Publishing.

Dr. Wilson has two grown daughters, an excellent son-in-law, and two outstanding grandsons. He lives in the Dutch Fork of South Carolina, not far from the Santee Swamp where Francis Marion and his men rested between raids on the first invader.

AVAILABLE FROM SHOTWELL

The Yankee Problem: An American Dilemma by Clyde N. Wilson (2016)

Maryland, My Maryland: The Cultural Cleansing of a Small Southern State by Joyce Bennett. (2016)

Washington's KKK: The Union League During Southern Reconstruction by John Chodes. (2016)

When the Yankees Come: Former South Carolina Slaves Remember Sherman's Invasion. Edited with Introduction by Paul C. Graham (2016)

Southerner, Take Your Stand! by John Vinson (2016)

Lies My Teacher Told Me: The True History of the War for Southern Independence by Clyde N. Wilson (2016)

Emancipation Hell: The Tragedy Wrought By Lincoln's Emancipation Proclamation by Kirkpatrick Sale (2015)

Southern Independence. Why War? - The War to Prevent Southern Independence by Dr. Charles T. Pace (2015)

IF YOU ENJOYED THIS BOOK or found it useful, interesting, or informative, we'd be very grateful if you would post a brief review of it on the retailer's website, Good Reads, Social Media, or anywhere else you think might help us get the word out.

In the current political and cultural climate, it is important that we get accurate, Southern friendly material into the hands of our friends and neighbours. *Your support can really make a difference* in helping us unapologetically celebrate and defend our Southern heritage, culture, history, and home!

For more information, or to sign-up for notification of forthcoming titles, please visit us at

www.ShotwellPublishing.com

THANK YOU FOR YOUR SUPPORT!

Made in the USA
San Bernardino, CA
09 April 2017